Lehrwerk für den Englischunterricht ab Klasse 3

Pupil's Book 3

Erarbeitet von
Jasmin Brune
Daniela Elsner
Stefanie Gleixner-Weyrauch
Marion Lugauer
Sabine Schwarz

Auf der Grundlage der Ausgabe von
Martina Bredenbröcker, Jasmin Brune,
Daniela Elsner, Barbara Gleich,
Stefanie Gleixner-Weyrauch,
Simone Gutwerk, Marion Lugauer,
Sabine Schwarz, Anke Spangenberg

Unter Beratung von
Jane Brockmann-Fairchild

Illustriert von
Barbara Jung, Wilfried Poll,
Sven Leberer, Anja Boretzki

Inhalt

What's your name?

① **Look and read:** My name is …

Susan   Tim   Emily   Phil   Eric   Liz

🔊 1 ② **Listen and sing.**

Good morning, hello! I am so happy.
Good morning, hello! How are you?

③ **Ask your partner:** What's your name? How are you?

English all around

(The illustration contains the following visible English words: sports and games, snowboard, OPEN, GILBERT, HOT DOGS, CHEESEBURGER, HAMBURGER, Coffee to go, Frozen Yoghurt, Smoothies, Muffins)

How are you, Emily?

Hi, Eric!

There is 1 🍔. There are 2 🍔🍔.

💬 ① There are many English words in the picture.
Look and say: I can see …

💬 ② Do you know more English words?

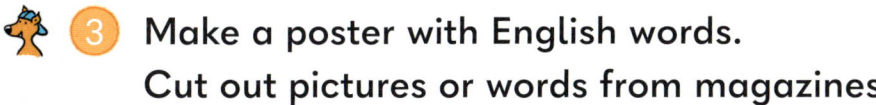

🐾 ③ Make a poster with English words.
Cut out pictures or words from magazines.

⭐ ④ Group the words (sports, food, drinks, …).

Mr Blue and Mrs Yellow

① Listen and point.

💬 ② What colour is it?

grey

pink

orange

purple

brown

green

 ③ Act out the story with a partner.

Make a video.

Sally's rhyme

 3 💬 (1) **Listen, say the rhyme and do the actions.**

One, two, three –
Sally, point to me!

Four, five, six –
Sally, let us mix!

Seven, eight, nine –
now let's stand in line!

Now comes ten,
let's say the rhyme again!

1   7   10   5   2   9   3   4   6   8

💬 (2) **Learn the rhyme.**

In class

① Listen and point.

pencil case

pencil

pen

ruler

book

schoolbag

Look at the board.

I've got an orange ruler.

My favourite book

Evic Phil

Emily

Tim

Liz

Sally's Dictionary

② **What school things have you got?**
Tell your partner: I've got a …

⭐ ③ **Make your own picture dictionary.**
Draw and write.

pen

I've got = I have got

School in England

 (1) **Talk about the pictures.**

> I can see …

> In the photo there is … / there are …

pupils in school uniform

a lollipop lady

lunchtime

assembly

	Monday	Tuesday	Wednesday	Thursday	Friday
9.15 – 9.30	Keep fit	Keep fit	Keep fit	Keep fit	Assembly
9.30 – 10.30	Maths	Literacy	Maths	Literacy	Drama
10.30 – 10.45	BREAK	BREAK	BREAK	BREAK	BREAK
10.45 – 12.15	Literacy	Maths	Literacy	Maths	Music
12.15 – 1.15	LUNCH	LUNCH	LUNCH	LUNCH	LUNCH
1.15 – 1.30	Silent reading	Silent reading	Silent reading	Silent reading	Silent reading
1.30 – 2.45	Art	Science	PE	Science	PE
2.45 – 3.15	Silent reading	Silent reading	PE	Silent reading	Silent reading
3.15 – 3.30	HOME	HOME	HOME	HOME	HOME

timetable

Ella's school day

① **Listen and read.**

My school day

Hello, my name is Ella.

I'm 9.

I go to Westminster School.

I'm in class 3c.

My teacher is Mrs Black.

My school uniform is red and white.

School starts at 9 o'clock in the morning

and ends at 4 o'clock in the afternoon.

I like music and sports.

What about you?

 ② **What about your school day?
Do a presentation.**

Make a video.

Checkpoint 1

> Good morning! How are you?

> Good morning! I'm fine, thanks.

8 1 2 7 9 5
3 10 6 4

> Hello! What's your name?

> My name is ...

> What colour is ...?

> It's ...

| schoolbag   pencil sharpener |
| book   rubber   pen   ruler |
| pencil case   pencil |

| blue   red   black   yellow   green |
| grey   pink   brown   orange   white |

1. **Look and speak.**
   There is ... / There are ... I can see ...

2. **What colours do you like?** I like ...

3. **Talk about your school things.**
   I've got 1 pen, 3 pencils, ...

4. **Point at a number.**
   Say the number. What colour is it?

Check your English

- Begrüße jemanden auf Englisch.
- Frage nach dem Namen.
- Stelle dich vor.
- Benenne Farben und frage danach.
- Benenne deine Schulsachen.

Head and shoulders

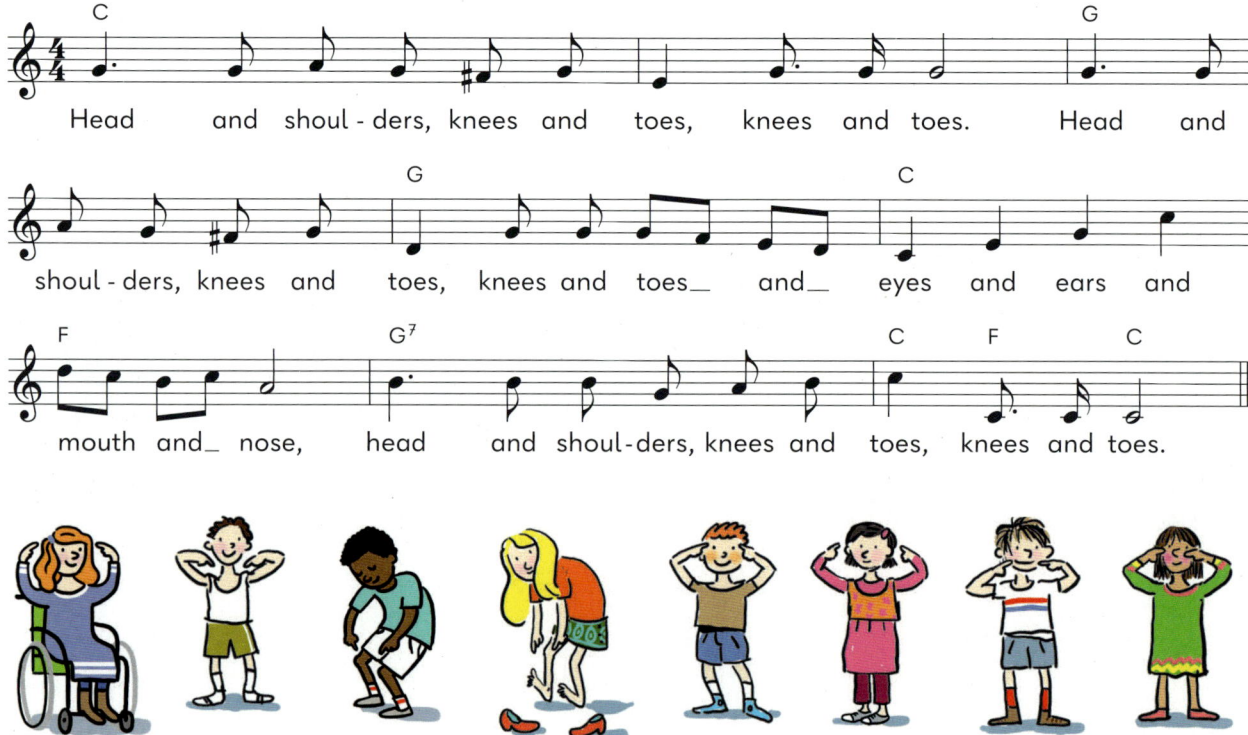

Head and shoul-ders, knees and toes, knees and toes. Head and shoul-ders, knees and toes, knees and toes_ and_ eyes and ears and mouth and_ nose, head and shoul-ders, knees and toes, knees and toes.

🔊 4 (1) Sing the song and do the actions.

(2) Sing the song faster and faster.

(3) Sing and drop the word [head].
Sing again and drop the words [head] and [shoulders] ...

Hm and shoulders, knees ...

Hm and hm, knees ...

one knee – two knees

AB 12 🔊 17

Ouch!

1 **Read the comic.**

Good morning, Sally. Here is your tea.

I can't go to school.

Let me see.

Ouch! My ears.

Go to school.

Let me see.

Ouch! My arm.

Go to school.

Ouch! My knee.

Let me see.

Sally, you are okay. Go to school.

2 **Act out the story.**

Make a video.

Snakes and ladders

1 Play the game. Do the actions.

Finish

64	63	62	61	60	59	58	57
49	50	52	53	54		56	
	51				55		
48	47	46	45	44	43	42	41
33	34	35	36	37	38	39	40
32	31	30	29	28	27	26	25
17	18	19	20	21		23	24
16	15	14	13	12	11 / 22	10	9
1	2	3	4	5	6	7	8

Start

It's my turn.

Roll the dice. Do the actions.

 Correct action 😊 : Go up the ladder.

 Wrong action 🙁 : Go down the snake.

 Sally's hotspot:

Correct action 😊 : Roll the dice again.

Wrong action 🙁 : Go back to the start.

one foot – two feet

3 Touch your head.

8 Bend your knees.

16 Sing: Head and shoulders …

19 Wash your hands.

24 Count your fingers.

27 Shake your feet.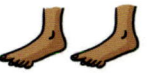

29 Stretch your arms.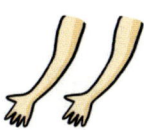

33 Point to your eyes.

43 Touch your ears.

48 Stretch your legs.

52 Brush your hair.

58 Say: Good morning!

59 Point to your nose.

62 Shake your body.

Monster, monster, how do you feel?

happy

angry

scared

sad

tired

💬 ① Listen, point and say: The yellow monster is ...

✂️ ✏️ ② Make a monster book.

⭐ ③ Which emojis do you know?
Draw and write.

Look it up on
the Internet.

Tim's wish list

spaceship £17 ⬜
helicopter £20 ✅
castle £30 ⬜
doll £17 ⬜
bike £100 £200 ✅
bike £90 ⬜
helmet £40 ✅
racing car £18 ⬜
ball £8 ⬜
helmet £30 ⬜
ruler £2 ⬜
rubber £1 ⬜
pencils £3 ⬜
book £5 ✅

1. Look at the toys. What does Tim want?
   Tell your partner: Tim wants **a** bike …

2. Ask your partner: How much is **the** …?

3. Make a wish list for your class and discuss.
   Use your dictionary.
   We want to buy …

I want –
Tim want**s**

Blue Monster wants it all!

Blue Monster loved brand new things more than anything. But soon he got bored.

"I don't want my old teddy bear, I want something new."

So his mom and dad gave him a baby sister. But soon he got bored.

"I don't want my old sister! I don't want my old teddy bear! Or my old mom and dad!"

He took all the money he got from his grandma and left home.

He bought a red sports car.
But the next day, Blue Monster
didn't like it.
"I don't want my old car!"

"What I really need is a new plane!"
So he bought a plane and flew off
to a tropical island...

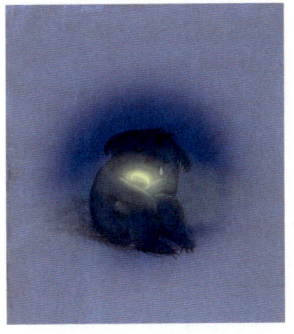

At night, Blue Monster was
scared and alone.
"I'll go and buy myself a
new family." But there were
no families for sale.

So Blue Monster flew all the way home
to give his old mom, his old dad, and
his old sister a good old hug.

1. **Listen and point.**

2. **Read the story.**

3. **What makes you happy?
   Tell your class.**

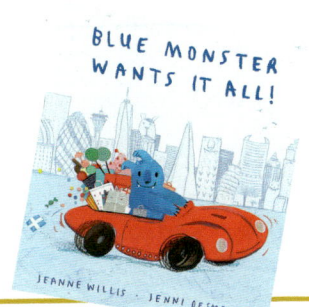

BLUE MONSTER
WANTS IT ALL!

JEANNE WILLIS · JENNI DESMOND

Sally in the snow

Sally, it's cold!

Sally, it's cold!!!

① Listen and point.

💬 ② Look and speak: Sally puts on her ... / Sally takes off her ...

💬 ③ **What are you wearing? Tell your partner: I'm wearing …**

⭐ ④ **Make a poster about winter clothes.**

What are they wearing?

> Hello, can you find me?
> I'm wearing a blue woolly hat, a red shirt, brown trousers and brown shoes.

> Hi, I'm wearing my favourite woolly hat. It's blue. I'm also wearing shorts, a white T-shirt and blue shoes. What colour are my shorts?

> Hi, I'm wearing a yellow dress, a red jacket, a red woolly hat and red shoes. What's my favourite colour?

> Hello, I'm wearing a yellow skirt, a blue T-shirt and blue shoes. Can you find me?

1. Listen and point. Find the children.

2. Read the speech bubbles.

3. Tell your partner: Who am I? Listen and point.
   Hi, I'm wearing ....

4. Do the clothes rally.

What's the weather like?

Thursday
Friday
Saturday
Wednesday
Sunday
Tuesday
Monday
Monday
Start
Tuesday
Finish
Wednesday
Saturday
Thursday
Friday
Friday
Thursday
Saturday
Wednesday
Sunday
Tuesday
Monday

Sally's week

What day is it?

It's Monday (Tuesday/…).

What's the weather like?

It's windy (sunny/…).

On Monday, it's windy.

Monday
Tuesday

① **Play the game:**
Roll the dice: What day is it? – It's Monday (Tuesday/…).
Roll the dice again: What's the weather like? –
It's windy (sunny/…). – On Monday, it's windy.

The wind and the sun

I'm stronger than you.

I'm stronger than you.

strong
stronger
strongest

1. Look at the picture. What can you see?

2. Listen to the story.

3. Act out the story in your group.

Make a video.

The weather forecast

London
Berlin
Rome
Istanbul
snowy
foggy
LONDON
BERLIN
windy, rainy
sunny
ROME
ISTANBUL
What's the weather like today?
Today it's …

1. Talk about the picture.
2. What's the weather like? Listen, point and tell.
3. What's the weather like in Paris, in Hamburg …? Make a weather forecast in your group and do a presentation.
4. Make a weather chart for one week.

Presentation tips:
- Speak loudly and clearly.
- Look at the class.
- Show pictures.

Look in a newspaper or on the Internet.

Checkpoint 2

How are you?

I'm ...

I'm ... And you?

I want the ... How much is the ...?

cold
Monday, Tuesday, Wednesday

hot
Thursday, Friday, Saturday, Sunday

Whether the weather is cold, whether the weather is hot, we have to put up with the weather, whether we like it or not.

It's £ ...

£6

£8

£4

£10

£9

£5

£2

£20

£10

dress   shirt   shoes   jeans
pullover   T-shirt   skirt   socks

happy   fine   sad   okay

doll   football   book   racing car   castle
helicopter   spaceship   bike   teddy bear

💬 ① **Look and speak.**

💬 ② **What are you wearing? Tell.**
I'm wearing ...

💬 ③ **Read and speak.**
cold – colder – ???
warm –   ???   – warmest
strong –   ???   – ???

Check your English

- Sage, wie du dich fühlst.
- Sage, welches Spielzeug du gerne hättest.
- Frage nach dem Preis.
- Beschreibe, wie das Wetter heute ist.
- Nenne die Wochentage.

AB 25

Happy birthday

Birthday invitation

Dear Susan,
Please come to my birthday party.

When: Saturday, 5 March at 2 o'clock
Where: 25, Main Street
Phone: 3472

Can you come to my party?
Yours, Emily

January	February	March 5 Emily
April	May	June
July	August	September
October	November	December

HAPPY BIRTHDAY

 1 Make a birthday calendar.

 **2** Talk about Emily's birthday party.

3 How do you celebrate your birthday?
Tell your class.

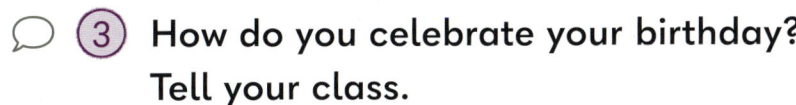 **4** Make a digital birthday invitation.

January
February

Keith Haring

the artist

"Best buddies"

"Football"

presentation

💬 ① **Look at the pictures.**
Describe the colours and actions.

 ② **Make a picture about friends:**
1. Cut out different figures.
2. Glue them on coloured paper.
3. Trace your figures with a black pen.

friend	orange	red
blue	purple	yellow
dance	play football	

My family

My mum and my dad play tennis.

My grandma and my grandpa like cats.

This is my family.

My brother Tim is 9 years old.

My aunt and my uncle like music.

This is my family.

Here are my mother,
my stepfather
and my stepsister Shari.

I have not got =
I haven't got

1 **Look and read.**

2 **What about your family? Tell:**
I've got ... / I haven't got ...

It's magic

Never do magic on your own!

Do magic to get me a cat.

Oh no! Marnie, where are you?

Please, help me!

Bubble, bubble, trick and track ...

I will never do magic on my own.

Make a video.

 ① Listen and point.

 ② Act out the story.

What is it?

💬 ① **Look and guess.**

tea   coke   orange juice   coffee
hot chocolate   milk

It's teatime

② **Listen and point.**

At the drinks stand

What would you like to drink?

I'd like a glass of water, please.

I'm thirsty.

1 Look and read.

 2 Make your own drinks stand.
Act out the scene.

 Make a video.

What's in your drink?

3 Read the text.

Drinking is very good for your body.
But not every drink is a healthy drink and good for you.
With one glass of coke you drink 12 sugar cubes.
A glass of orange juice contains 11 sugar cubes.
With one glass of lemonade you drink 13 sugar cubes.
But there are drinks with no sugar at all. Guess!

 Use your dictionary or the Internet.

 4 Make a poster about drinks.

The magic trick

1 Do the trick.

2 Can you do a magic trick? Show your class.

⭐ 3 Do you know more food and drink words? Tell your partner.

1 orange juice	8 hot chocolate
2 honey	9 jam
3 tea	10 cheese
4 toast	11 egg
5 ham	12 coffee
6 water	13 milk
7 bread	14 roll
	15 cornflakes

A traditional English breakfast

① **Listen and point.**

② **Guess what happened.**

③ **What is a traditional breakfast in your family? Tell.**

My favourite breakfast

  Look and speak.

everyday breakfast

traditional breakfast

  Ask your partner.

Do you like ... on your / in your ... ?

Do you like ...?

Yes, I do.

No, I don't.

  **Make your own split-up book.**

 **Do the breakfast rally.**

Checkpoint 3

January	February	March
April	May	June
July	August	September
October	November	December

Happy birthday!

When's your birthday?

My birthday is in …

How old are you?

I'm …

💬 ① **Look and speak.**

💬 ② **How many brothers and sisters have you got?**
I've got … / I haven't got any …

💬 ③ **What drinks do you like?**
I like … / I don't like …

💬 ④ **What do you have for breakfast?**
For breakfast, I have …

bread   butter   cheese   eggs
ham   tea   water   hot chocolate

Check your English

- Sage, wann du Geburtstag hast.
- Frage jemanden nach seinem Alter.
- Gratuliere jemandem zum Geburtstag.
- Frage ein anderes Kind, wie viele Geschwister es hat.
- Sage, wer zu deiner Familie gehört.
- Sage, was du gerne zum Frühstück isst und trinkst.

At the ice cream stand

Can I help you?

cherry

banana

pear

vanilla

chocolate

lemon

strawberry

orange

pineapple

I'd like …

Let's have
an ice cream.

 **1** **Listen and speak.**

2 **Ask your partner:**
What's your favourite ice cream?

Ice cream rock

 7 （1） **Listen. Read and sing the song.**

I scream, you scream, we scream for ice cream. You

scream, they scream, we scream for ice cream.

1. One scoop of or - ange, one scoop of plum,
2. One scoop of ap - ple, one scoop of pear,

one scoop of cher - ry, one scoop of le - mon.
one scoop of choco - late, one scoop of me - lon.

1, 2, 3, 4 ice cream, 1, 2, 3, 4 ice cream!

（2） **Read the riddles. Find the fruit.**

> It's sweet and red. It has a green hat.

> It's soft and yellow.

> It's round and green or red.

| sour sweet soft |
| hard round small big |

| purple yellow orange |
| red green brown |

 （3） **Make your own riddle.**

 （4） **Make a wordweb.**

yellow — fruit — sour: lemon

round: apple, orange, ...

Let's make a smoothie!

1 Listen, point and read.

This is what you need.

Wash the strawberries.

Peel the bananas.

Cut the fruit.

Put them into the jug.

Add water or milk.

Mix it.

Pour the smoothie into your glass.

Enjoy!

Make a video.

 2 Create your own smoothie.

My favourite pet

(1) **Read the riddles. Which pet is it?**

> My pets are blue with yellow heads.
> My pets are little.

> My pet is grey.
> It has got orange eyes.
> It's hairy.
> It has got a long tail.

> My pet is grey.
> It is little and hairy.
> Its name is Speedy.

> My pet is big.
> It has got a long tail and little ears.
> Its name is Charly.
> Charly is black.

> My pet is black.
> It has got long ears and a little tail.
> I love Hopsy.

Little dog lost

Playing in the garden …	Looking for Bobby …
	In the animal centre …

In the story posters:

Little dog lost
→ We miss Bobby

Little dog lost
→ We miss Bobby very much.
Tim and Susan Brown
phone: 9856

1 **Listen. Where is Bobby?**

London

The wheels on the bus

1. The wheels on the bus go round and round,
round and round, round and round.
The wheels on the bus go round and round,
all around the town.

2. The wipers on the bus
go swish, swish, swish …

beep beep

3. The horn on the bus goes beep, beep, beep …

Move on back!

4. The driver on the bus says "Move on back!" …

Wah!

5. The baby on the bus says "Wah, wah, wah!" …

Shh …

6. The mummy on the bus says "Shh, shh, shh" …

 9 ① **Listen, sing and act it out.**

Sing and record.

⭐ ② **Write your own verse. Use your dictionary.**

42 forty-two

62

The Tower of London

The crowns of the King and the Queen and all the crown jewels are in the Tower.

In the Tower you can see armour, swords and other weapons.

There was a prison in the Tower. It was cold, dark and stinky.

The ravenmaster feeds the seven ravens.

Come here, I've got some food for you.

1 Listen, look and read.

2 Do the quiz.

 **London**

Let's go to London!

the Royal Family: King Charles and Queen Camilla,
William, Kate and their children

Buckingham Palace   Tower Bridge

London Eye   Big Ben   guards

Find information
on the Internet.

 Look at the photos.

 Make a poster about London sights.

44 forty-four   AB 43

Alphabet rhyme

A B C D E F G,
on the farm there is a bee.

H I J K L M N,
it lands directly on a hen.

How are you?

O P Q R S T U,
and asks her friendly:
"How are you?"

Get off my head!

V W X Y Z,
"I'm fine, but please,
get off my head."

🔊 10 ① **Listen and point.**

② **Read the rhyme.**

③ **Do the animal rally.**

Record the rhyme.

Clumsy the dog

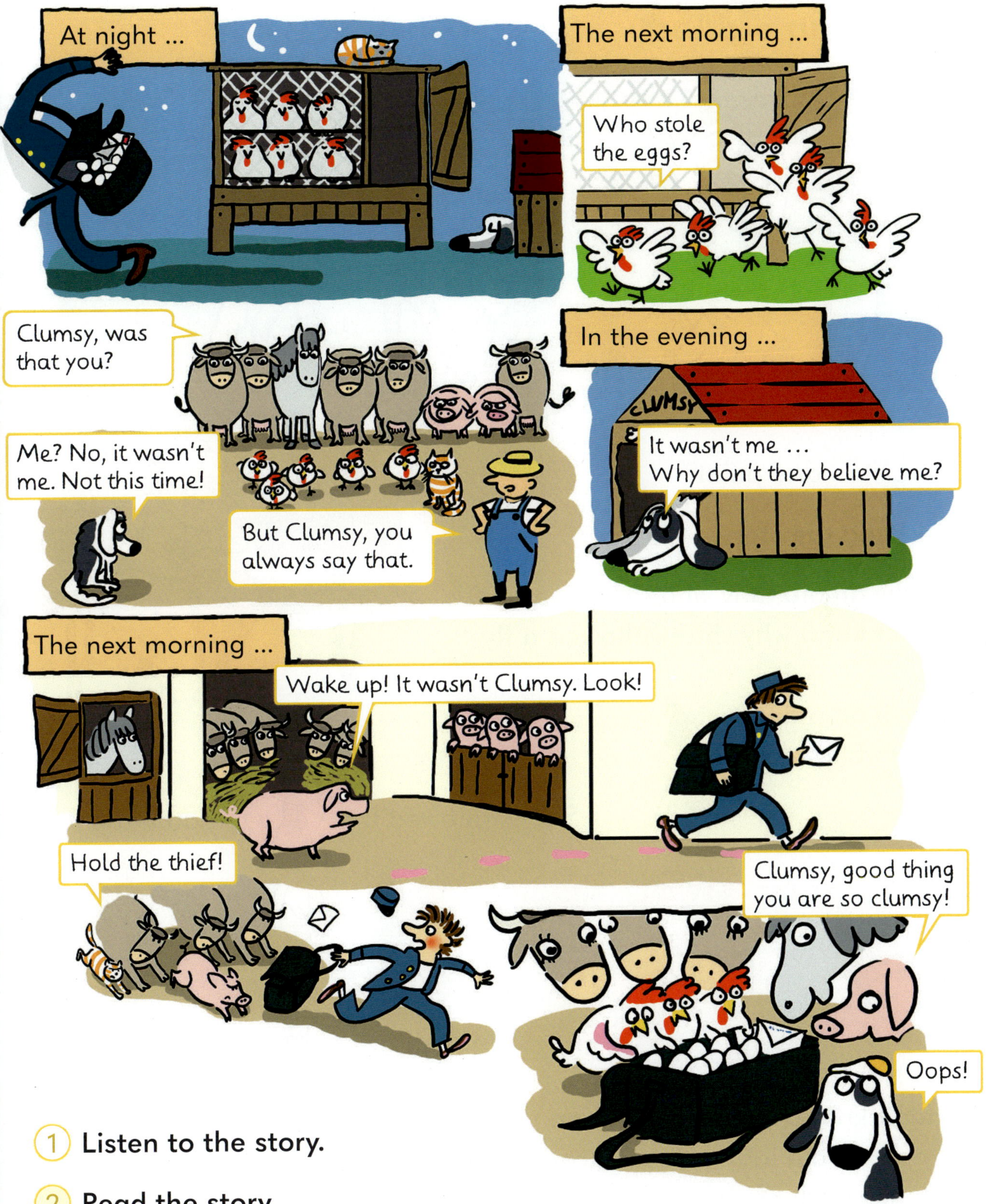

At night ...

The next morning ...

Who stole the eggs?

Clumsy, was that you?

In the evening ...

CLUMSY

It wasn't me ... Why don't they believe me?

Me? No, it wasn't me. Not this time!

But Clumsy, you always say that.

The next morning ...

Wake up! It wasn't Clumsy. Look!

Hold the thief!

Clumsy, good thing you are so clumsy!

Oops!

1 **Listen to the story.**

2 **Read the story.**

I know an old lady ...

(1) **Listen and point.**

(2) **Read the story:**

I know an old lady who swallowed a fly.
I don't know why she swallowed a fly.

I know an old lady
who swallowed a  .

 . She swallowed the  to catch the fly.

 .   .

 .   .    .

                                           . 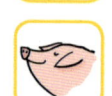 .

I don't know why she swallowed the fly.
I know an old lady who swallowed a horse – and then?
She sneezed, of course!!!

Checkpoint 4

Speech bubbles in the illustration:
- Can I help you?
- Here you are. That's £ ..., please.
- Yes. I'd like 1 scoop of ...
- Thank you. Goodbye.
- 1 scoop = £1
- apple / strawberry / plum / orange / chocolate
- ICE CREAM
- strawberries / apples / plums

💬 **1** **Look and speak.**

💬 **2** **Which fruit do you like?**
Which fruit don't you like?
I like ... / I don't like ...

💬 **3** **Cover the words.**
How many animals can you name in 15 seconds?

cat	pig	cow	dog	fish
duck	goose	hen	hamster	
horse	mouse	rabbit	sheep	
guinea pig	tortoise			

💬 **4** **What's your favourite ice cream?**
My favourite ice cream is ... and ...

💬 **5** **Spell these animal words.**

Check your English

- Benenne und beschreibe einige Früchte.
- Bestelle ein Eis.
- Benenne und beschreibe einige Tiere.

Robin Hood's clever trick

1 Listen and point.

2 Read the story.

3 **Act out the story.**

It's Halloween

Boo!

The ghost
I saw a ghost.
He saw me, too.
I waved at him.
But he said "Boo!".

Tongue twister
Two witches are watching two watches.
Which witch is watching which watch?

💬 ① Look and read.
Can you say the tongue twister?

⭐ ② Find more Halloween rhymes or tongue twisters.

Emily's costume

> What a dark night.

> Look, there's Emily's house.

> Oh no, there's a bat. I hate bats.

> Trick or treat!

> Oh no, there's a monster behind the bush. I hate monsters.

🔊 12 (1) **Listen to the song.**

(2) **Listen to the story.**

⭐ (3) **Act out the story.**

> I don't hate bats. I love them.

Christmas Eve

Ho, ho, ho!

I wish you a Merry Christmas and a happy New Year.

① Listen to the story.

💬 ② How do you celebrate Christmas?

🔊14 ③ Sing the song. Act it out.

Hurry, Santa!

It is Christmas Eve.
"Hurry, Santa!"

Santa puts on his clothes.

"Go, reindeer, go!"
"Oooooh!" CRASH!

"We did it!" says Santa
back at the North Pole.

"Oh no! I've forgotten someone!"

"That present is for you.
It's Christmas Day!"

① **Listen and point.**

② **Read the story.**

③ **What is Santa's Christmas present? Guess.**

Make your own Christmas stocking

You need:
thick brown paper, a pencil,
scissors, glue, a hole punch,
wool, felt tips or wax crayons
and coloured paper

1 Draw a large stocking
on the thick brown paper.

2 Cut out two copies
of the stocking.

3 Glue the two stockings
together around the edges.
Leave the top open.

4 Punch holes around
the edges of the stocking.

5 Weave wool in and out
of the holes.

6 Leave a loop of wool.
Tie it into a knot.
Decorate your stocking.

1. **Look and read.**

  2. **Create your own stocking.**

3. **Describe your stocking:**
   On my stocking there is/are …

| star | tree | candle |

Valentine's cards

① **Read the comic.**

② **Read the rhymes. What's your favourite rhyme?**

In February
it's Valentine's Day.
I write Valentine's cards
to my friends.

Jingle, jangle,
silver bangle,
you look fit
from every angle.

Candy is sweet,
this is true,
but for my Valentine
I'll choose you.

I like you!
Be my Valentine!

Roses are red,
violets are blue,
sugar is sweet
and so are you!

  ③ **Make your own Valentine's card.**

Edgar's Easter eggs

There is …

 There are …

1. Talk about the pictures.

I can see … → I like …

2. Listen to the story.

3. Make your own Easter egg cup.

AB 56, 57 🔊 93 ▶

Grammar rules and Words

a cherry – a banana
an apple – an orange

I want to read a book.
I want to read the book about "Blue Monster".

There is 1 🍔.
There are 2 🍔🍔.

1 dog – 2 dogs
1 cat – 2 cats

1 mouse – 2 mice
1 goose – 2 geese
1 fish – 2 fish

I like ... 🙂
I don't like ... 🙁

I want –
Tim wants

I've got =
I have got

I haven't got =
I have not got

he she it

my pen
your pen
his pen
her pen

Monday
Tuesday

January
February

strong
stronger
strongest

in on under
in front of behind
next to between

in

on

under

in front of

behind

next to

between

Tips and tricks: How to learn English words

Read the word out loud
three times.

Draw a picture.
Write the word next to it.

Read the word.
Cover it and say the word.
Check.

Use the word in a sentence.
Write it down.

Make a mindmap.

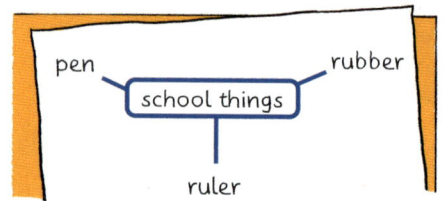

Hello
Hallo

boy   Junge
girl   Mädchen
children   Kinder

basketball   Basketball
computer game   Computerspiel
mobile phone   Handy
inline skating   Inlineskaten
singing   Singen
skateboard   Skateboard
tennis   Tennis

Hello. / Hi.   Hallo.

Good morning.   Guten Morgen.

How are you? – I'm fine, thanks.
Wie geht es dir? – Danke, gut.

What's your name? – My name is …
Wie heißt du? – Ich heiße …

What do you like? –
I like … And you?
Was magst du? –
Ich mag … Und du?

I can see (a) …   Ich sehe (ein/e) …

There is … / There are …
Da ist … / Da sind …

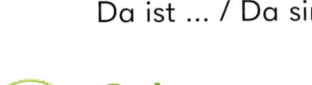

Colours and numbers
Farben und Zahlen

black   schwarz
blue   blau
brown   braun
green   grün
grey   grau
orange   orange

pink   rosa, pink
purple   lila
red   rot
white   weiß
yellow   gelb

one   eins
two   zwei
three   drei
four   vier
five   fünf
six   sechs
seven   sieben
eight   acht
nine   neun
ten   zehn

What colour is it? –
It's green (blue …).
Welche Farbe hat es? –
Es ist grün (blau …).

What's your telephone/mobile
number? – My telephone/mobile
number is …
Wie lautet deine Telefonnummer/
Handynummer? – Meine Telefon-
nummer/Handynummer ist …

At school
In der Schule

board   Tafel
book   Buch
class   Klasse
classroom   Klassenzimmer
computer   Computer
folder   Ordner
glue stick   Klebestift
lollipop lady   Schülerlotsin
pen   Füller
pencil   Bleistift

pencil case   Federmäppchen
pencil sharpener   Spitzer
pupil   Schüler(in)
rubber   Radiergummi
ruler   Lineal
school   Schule
schoolbag   Schultasche
school things   Schulsachen
school uniform   Schuluniform
(a pair of) scissors   eine Schere
teacher   Lehrer(in)

in   in
on   auf
under   unter

I've got a ...   Ich habe ein(e, en) ...

I go to Westminster School.
Ich gehe in die Westminster-Schule.

I'm in class 3c.
Ich bin in der Klasse 3c.

My teacher is Mrs/Mr ...
Meine Lehrerin / Mein Lehrer
heißt Frau/Herr ...

Body and feelings
Körper und Gefühle

arm   Arm
body   Körper
ear   Ohr
eye   Auge
face   Gesicht
finger   Finger
foot – feet   Fuß – Füße
hair   Haar
hand   Hand
head   Kopf
knee   Knie
leg   Bein

monster   Monster
mouth   Mund
nose   Nase
shoulder   Schulter
toe   Zeh
tooth – teeth   Zahn – Zähne

angry   zornig
because   weil
fine   gut
happy   glücklich
sad   traurig
scared   verängstigt, erschrocken
tired   müde

How do you feel? – I'm happy/sad ...
Wie fühlst du dich? – Ich bin
glücklich/traurig ...
I'm okay.   Mir geht's gut.

Toys
Spielzeug

big   groß
bike   Fahrrad
car   Auto
castle   Burg, Schloss
children   Kinder
computer game   Computerspiel
doll   Puppe
football   Fußball
helicopter   Hubschrauber
helmet   Helm
playing cards   Spielkarten
racing car   Rennauto
small   klein
spaceship   Raumschiff
teddy bear   Teddybär

(to) want   wollen
(to) wish (for)   sich wünschen

eleven   elf
twelve   zwölf
thirteen   dreizehn
fourteen   vierzehn
fifteen   fünfzehn
sixteen   sechzehn
seventeen   siebzehn
eighteen   achtzehn
nineteen   neunzehn
twenty   zwanzig

British   britisch
money   Geld
penny – pence (p)   Penny – Pence
pound (£)   Pfund

How much is the ...? –
The ... is ... pounds.
Wie viel kostet der (die, das) ...? –
Der (die, das) ... kostet ... Pfund.

How much is it? – It's ... pounds.
Wie viel kostet das? – Es kostet ...
Pfund.

Tim/Susan wants ...
Tim/Susan möchte ...

Clothes
Kleidung

boots   Stiefel
cap   Kappe
coat   Mantel
dress   Kleid
gloves   Handschuhe
jacket   Jacke
(a pair of) jeans   eine Jeans
pullover   Pullover
(to) put on   anziehen
scarf   Schal
shirt   Hemd

shoes   Schuhe
(a pair of) shorts
eine kurze Hose, Shorts
skirt   Rock
socks   Socken
(to) take off   ausziehen
(a pair of) trousers   eine Hose
T-shirt   T-Shirt
(to) wear   tragen, anhaben
woolly hat   Mütze

For my holidays, I pack ...
Für meine Ferien packe ich ... ein.

Sally puts on her ... / takes off her ...
Sally zieht ihr(e, en) ... an/aus.

Weather and days
Wetter und Tage

Monday   Montag
Tuesday   Dienstag
Wednesday   Mittwoch
Thursday   Donnerstag
Friday   Freitag
Saturday   Samstag
Sunday   Sonntag
day   Tag
week   Woche

cloud/y   Wolke/wolkig
cold   kalt
fog/gy   Nebel/neblig
hot   heiß
rain/y   Regen/regnerisch
snow/y   Schnee/verschneit
strong   stark
sun/ny   Sonne/sonnig
warm   warm
weather forecast   Wettervorhersage
wind/y   Wind/windig

When can we meet? – We can meet
on Monday (Tuesday …).
Wann können wir uns treffen? –
Wir können uns am Montag (Dienstag …) treffen.

What day is it? – It's Monday.
(Tuesday …).   Welchen Tag haben
wir? – Es ist Montag (Dienstag …).

What's the weather like today? –
Today it's windy (sunny …).
Wie ist das Wetter heute? –
Heute ist es windig (sonnig …).

On Monday, it's sunny.
Am Montag ist es sonnig.

Around the year
Rund ums Jahr

January   Januar
February   Februar
March   März
April   April
May   Mai
June   Juni
July   Juli
August   August
September   September
October   Oktober
November   November
December   Dezember
month   Monat

spring   Frühling
summer   Sommer
autumn   Herbst
winter   Winter
season   Jahreszeit

balloon   Ballon
birthday   Geburtstag
cake   Torte, Kuchen
calendar   Kalender
candle   Kerze
card   Karte
crown   Krone
guest   Gast
invitation   Einladung
party   Party, Feier
present   Geschenk

When's your birthday? –
My birthday is in …
Wann ist dein Geburtstag? –
Mein Geburtstag ist im …

Happy birthday!
Alles Gute zum Geburtstag!

How old are you? –
I'm eight (years old).
Wie alt bist du? –
Ich bin acht (Jahre alt).

Family and friends
Familie und Freunde

aunt   Tante
boy   Junge
brother   Bruder
family   Familie
father/dad   Vater/Papa
friend   Freund(in)
girl   Mädchen
grandfather/grandpa
Großvater/Opa
grandmother/grandma
Großmutter/Oma
mother/mum   Mutter/Mama
sister   Schwester

stepbrother   Stiefbruder
stepfather   Stiefvater
stepmother   Stiefmutter
stepsister   Stiefschwester
uncle   Onkel

My best friend is ...
Mein(e) beste(r) Freund(in) ist ...

He/She is ... years old.
Er/Sie ist ... Jahre alt.

He/She has got ...   Er/Sie hat ...

Have you got brothers or sisters? –
I've got ... / I haven't got any ...
Hast du Geschwister? –
Ich habe ... / Ich habe keine ...

This is my family. /
These are my friends.
Das ist meine Familie. /
Dies sind meine Freunde.

Drinks
Getränke

coffee   Kaffee
coke   Cola
hot chocolate   Kakao
lemonade   Limonade
(a glass of) milk   (ein Glas) Milch
orange juice   Orangensaft
(a cup of) tea   (eine Tasse) Tee
teatime   Teezeit
water   Wasser

healthy   gesund
sugar cubes   Zuckerwürfel
unhealthy   ungesund

What drinks do you like? – I like ...
Welche Getränke magst du? –
Ich mag ...

I like ... best.   Am liebsten mag ich
...

What drinks don't you like? –
I don't like ...
Welche Getränke magst du nicht? –
Ich mag kein(e, en) ...

What would you like to drink? –
I'd like ..., please.   Was würdest du
gerne trinken? – Ich hätte gerne ...,
bitte.

Breakfast
Frühstück

baked beans   gebackene Bohnen
bread   Brot
breakfast   Frühstück
butter   Butter
cheese   Käse
cornflakes   Cornflakes
(to) drink   trinken
(to) eat   essen
egg   Ei
fried egg   Spiegelei
fried tomatoes   gebratene Tomaten
ham   Schinken
honey   Honig
jam   Marmelade
ketchup   Ketchup
roll   Brötchen
salt   Salz
sausages   Würstchen
sugar   Zucker
toast   Toast

What do you have for breakfast?
Was isst/trinkst du zum Frühstück?

For breakfast, I have ...
Zum Frühstück esse/trinke ich ...

Do you like ...? –
Yes, I do. / No, I don't.
Magst du ...? – Ja. / Nein.

Can I have the ..., please? –
Here you are.   Kann ich bitte den/
die/das ... haben? – Hier, bitte.

Fruit
Obst

apple   Apfel
banana   Banane
cherry   Kirsche
fruit   Frucht, Obst
lemon   Zitrone
melon   Melone
orange   Orange, Apfelsine
pear   Birne
pineapple   Ananas
plum   Pflaume
strawberry   Erdbeere
tree   Baum

big   groß
hard   hart
round   rund
small   klein
soft   weich
sour   sauer
sweet   süß

(to) add   hinzufügen
(to) cut   schneiden
ice cream   Eiscreme
ice cream stand   Eisstand

jug   Krug
(to) mix   mischen
(to) peel   schälen
(to) pour   eingießen
(to) put   hineingeben, legen, stellen
scoop   Eiskugel
smoothie   Smoothie, Fruchtshake
(to) wash   waschen

What's your favourite ice cream?
Was ist dein Lieblingseis?

Can I help you?
Kann ich dir/euch/Ihnen helfen?

I'd like ... – Here you are.
Ich hätte gerne ... – Hier, bitte.

That's ... pounds, please. – Thank you.
Das macht bitte ... Pfund. – Danke.

Goodbye.   Auf Wiedersehen.

Pets
Haustiere

animal centre   Tierheim
bird   Vogel
budgie   Wellensittich
cat   Katze
dog   Hund
fish   Fisch(e)
guinea pig   Meerschweinchen
hamster   Hamster
mouse – mice   Maus – Mäuse
pet   Haustier
rabbit   Kaninchen
tail   Schwanz
tortoise   Schildkröte
wing   Flügel

(too) dirty (zu) schmutzig
(too) hairy (zu) haarig/behaart
(too) little (zu) klein
(too) loud (zu) laut

Have you got a pet? – Yes, I have
got a ... / No, I haven't got a pet.
Hast du ein Haustier? – Ja, ich habe
ein ... / Nein, ich habe kein Haustier.

What's your favourite pet? –
My favourite pet is a ...
Was ist dein Lieblingshaustier? –
Mein Lieblingshaustier ist ein(e) ...

Its name is ... Es heißt ...

Can I help you? – I've lost my pet.
Kann ich dir/euch/Ihnen helfen? –
Ich habe mein Haustier verloren.

What colour is it? – It's black
(brown ...).
Welche Farbe hat es? – Es ist
schwarz (braun ...).

London
London

(double-decker) bus
(Doppeldecker-)Bus
bus driver Busfahrer
crown Krone
crown jewels Kronjuwelen
England England
(to) feed füttern
guard Wache, Wachposten
king König
(to) move bewegen, sich bewegen
palace Palast
prince Prinz
princess Prinzessin

prison Gefängnis
queen Königin
raven Rabe
raven master Rabenmeister
Royal Family Königsfamilie
set of armour Rüstung
sight Sehenswürdigkeit
sword Schwert
weapon Waffe

I want to be a ... Ich will ein(e) ...
sein.

I want to see ... Ich will ... sehen.

Farm animals
Bauernhoftiere

animal Tier
barn Stall
bee Biene
clumsy ungeschickt
cow Kuh
duck Ente
farm Bauernhof
farmer Bauer
goose – geese Gans – Gänse
hen Huhn, Henne
horse Pferd
pig Schwein
pond Teich
roof Dach
sheep Schaf, Schafe

behind hinter
between zwischen
in in
in front of vor
next to neben
on auf
under unter

What's your favourite animal? –
It's a ...
Was ist dein Lieblingstier? –
Es ist ein(e) ...

Where is the ...? – It's in/on/under/
behind/in front of/next to/between
the ...
Wo ist ...? – Es ist in/auf/unter/hinter/
vor/neben/zwischen ...

My animal is ... / It's ...
Mein Tier ist ... / Es ist ein/eine ...

My animal/It has got ...
Mein Tier/Es hat ...

Robin Hood
Robin Hood

arrow   Pfeil
bow   Bogen
castle   Burg, Schloss
(to) catch   fangen
(to) dress up   sich verkleiden
forest   Wald
hat   Hut
(to) play a trick
einen Streich spielen
poor   arm
rich   reich
(to) ride (a horse)
(ein Pferd) reiten
sheriff   Sheriff
(to) shoot   schießen

Help!   Hilfe!

Hands up!   Hände hoch!

Happy Halloween
Fröhliches Halloween

bat   Fledermaus
broom   Besen
costume   Kostüm, Verkleidung
dark   dunkel
door   Tür
ghost   Geist, Gespenst
Halloween   Halloween
hat   Hut
house   Haus
(to) knock   klopfen
monster   Ungeheuer, Monster
moon   Mond
night   Nacht
pumpkin   Kürbis
(to) shake   schütteln
skeleton   Gerippe, Skelett
star   Stern
sweets   Süßigkeiten
vampire   Vampir
witch   Hexe

Happy Halloween!
Fröhliches Halloween!

It's eight (nine ...) o'clock.
Es ist acht (neun ...) Uhr.

Trick or treat!
Süßes oder Saures!

Merry Christmas
Frohe Weihnachten

bell   Glocke
carrot   Karotte
chimney   Schornstein
Christmas card   Weihnachtskarte

Christmas Day
(erster) Weihnachtstag
Christmas Eve   Heiligabend,
Weihnachtsabend
Christmas tree   Weihnachtsbaum
Father Christmas   Weihnachts-
mann
fireplace   (offener) Kamin
(to) get presents   Geschenke
bekommen
hungry   hungrig
mistletoe   Mistel(zweig)
reindeer   Rentier(e)
sleigh   Schlitten
snowman   Schneemann
stocking   Strumpf

Merry Christmas!   Frohe Weihnachten!

I wish you a happy New Year!
Ich wünsche dir ein frohes neues
Jahr!

Valentine's Day
Valentinstag

Valentine's Day   Valentinstag

(to) write Valentine's cards
Valentinskarten schreiben

It's Valentine's Day.
Es ist Valentinstag.

I like you.   Ich mag dich.

Happy Easter
Frohe Ostern

basket   Korb
bush   Busch
(to) colour   färben, anmalen
Easter bunny   Osterhase
Easter egg   Osterei
Easter egg cup   Ostereierbecher
fence   Zaun
fun   Spaß
happy   glücklich
(to) hide   verstecken
sad   traurig
(to) share   teilen

behind   hinter
in   in
in front of   vor
on   auf
under   unter

Happy Easter!   Frohe Ostern!

Is the yellow (red ...) egg in/on/under
the ...?
Ist das gelbe (rote ...) Ei in/auf/unter
dem/der ...?

9   Fotos: (ob. li.) mauritius images / alamy stock photo / Peter Titmuss; (ob. re.) mauritius images / Angela Hampton Picture Library / Alamy; (un. li.) Monkey Business Images / Shutterstock.com; (un. re.) Imago Stock & People GmbH / ZUMA Press

10   mauritius images / alamy stock photo / Avril O'Reilly

18/19   Extracts from Blue Monster Wants It All! text copyright © Jeanne Willis 2018, illustration copyright © Jenni Desmond 2018. Published by Little Tiger Press, London.

28   Fotos: (ob. li.) Self-portrait Polaroid circa 1980; (ob. re.) Best Buddies, 1990; (un. li.) Untitled, 1988: alle © The Keith Haring Foundation. Used by permission; (un. re.) Marion Lugauer, Erding

31   (ob. li.) Natalia V. Guseva / Shutterstock.com; (ob. Mi.) Pixelspieler / Shutterstock.com; (ob. re.) Victor Masalski / Shutterstock.com; (un. li.) Degtiarova Viktoriia / Shutterstock.com; (un. Mi.) Valentyn Volkov / Shutterstock.com; (un. re.) focal point / Shutterstock.com

39   Fotos: Stefanie Gleixner-Weyrauch, München

42   Foto: Chris Jenner / Shutterstock.com

44   Fotos: (ob. li.) dpa Picture-Alliance / Photoshot; (ob. re.) dpa Picture-Alliance / empics / PA Wire / Chris Jackson; (Mi. li.) Monkey Business Images / Shutterstock.com; (Mi. re.) stocker1970 / Shutterstock.com; (un. li.) m.page/Shutterstock.com; (un. Mi.) Nella/Shutterstock.com; (un. re.) KimPinPhotography / Shutterstock.com

55   Extracts from Hurry, Santa! text copyright © Julie Sykes 1998, illustration copyright © Tim Warnes 1998. Published by Little Tiger Press, London.

56   Fotos: Cornelsen / Johann Jilka, Altenstadt

57   Fotos: Marion Lugauer, Erding

58   Foto: Cornelsen / Heiko Jegodtka, München